God, I'm Listening

Jim Kay

ISBN: 1500483265

ISBN-13: 978-1500483265

DEDICATION

To my wife Jenna and three children, Madison, Noah, and Catera

What this book is about

A young girl named Lilyana asks her dad how God speaks to people. She wants to be able to talk with God and hear his advice. Near bedtime, the two of them talk about how Lily can hear God.

Lily's dad called from down the hall. "Lily, its bedtime. Are your teeth brushed yet?"

Lily had just taken her dark brown hair out of her ponytail and was brushing it when she heard her dad. She called back, "Yep, all done. I'm ready to be tucked in."

"Let me see those pearly white teeth of yours." Lily's dad glanced at her just-brushed teeth, and then ran his fingers down her back. "Your hair is getting long. Are you going to donate it again?"

Lily smiled, remembering how she felt the first time she'd donated twelve inches of her hair for people going through cancer treatment. "I think I'll let it grow enough to donate it and then start all over. I can grow it out again and again."

"Well you do have the prettiest hair. I'm sure it's in high demand, my munchkin. I bet God is very happy for your help."

Her dad gave Lily's hair a bit of a tug. "Does pulling it like this make it grow?"

"Dad, don't be a silly goose." Lily climbed into bed. "I have a really important question. I've been thinking a lot about this and want to know the truth."

Her dad's face got serious. "What's your question?"

Lily pulled the covers up where she liked them, looked up at her father and asked, "How does God talk to people?"

"Oh, that really is a serious question. Let me see . . ." Her dad sat at the edge of her bed, nudging her with his hip to make room. "God has used angels, regular people, the Bible, prophets, dreams, and visions."

"But Dad . . . what I really want . . . I want to know if God talks to anyone, like anyone, anyone?"

"Of course He can. God can do anything. God can talk to anyone no matter where they live, from the North Pole to the South Pole."

Lily fidgeted her legs under the covers and asked, "Does He only talk to people who go to church?"

"No, honey. God will talk with anyone. But having a relationship with Him helps, and going to church helps you build that relationship."

"Why?" Lily asked.

"You and your brother have a bond because you spend time together. If you didn't spend time with Jacob, he wouldn't ask you for advice. Because you have a relationship, you two can talk back and forth. Church and prayer are where you spend time with God and learn to talk together."

Lily scrunched up her face as she puzzled that out.

Her dad smiled at her. "Relationships are a two-way street. You won't hear from people you don't know well. Think about it this way . . . you don't know my boss. He wouldn't call you out of the blue. But if you had a relationship with him, he might call you." Her dad paused for a second. "If my boss ever does call you, tell him I deserve a pay raise."

"Don't be goofy. What I need to know is . . . can God really speak to people?"

"Yes. In the book of Genesis, God walked and spoke with Adam and Eve. God gave them advice about the right way to live." Genesis 3

"That's the type of relationship I want God and me to have. I want to hear his advice." Lily hugged her pillow and wiggled her face into it, as if she was giving it a hug.

"Another time, Jesus' father Joseph was thinking about breaking his engagement with Mary. She had told him she was going to have a baby, and Joseph thought she was lying. But lucky for us, God sent an angel. The angel told Joseph to marry Mary."

"Marry Mary; marry Mary."

"You're so cute. But think about it . . . Jesus' birth would have been very different if He was born to a single mother with no father." Matthew 1:18-25

Lily smiled and said, "That's so cool. I want an angel to visit and help me with my problems."

"Would you listen to an angel? You don't listen when I ask you to clean your room."

"I clean my room. You're just too picky!" Lily looked around. "Maybe my angel could help me clean up better."

"You would need an angel to make this room clean." He crinkled his nose. "And maybe smell better too."

Lily laughed.

Her Dad tweaked her chin with his fingers. "But did you know that Joseph saw another angel? Baby Jesus' life was in danger. A bad man named King Herod was planning on killing little baby Jesus. But an angel warned Joseph to get his family out of town." Matthew 2:13

"That's cool." Lily sat up in bed a bit. "I wish an angel had warned me before that bully pushed me down on the playground."

"Yeah, King Herod and your bully would probably be good friends . . . if they hadn't been born thousands of years apart. But another awesome angel visit is described in the book of Acts. An angel visited the leader of some soldiers. The angel gave clear instructions to send a group of men and pick up a guy named Simon Peter. The angel even told the soldier which house to visit. Simon Peter returned with the soldiers and Simon preached that they could eat pork, which had been against the rules for a long time. Simon Peter knew this because God had given him a detailed dream about what people could eat and even how to preach this message." Acts 10

"So you're telling me that I get to eat bacon because God told some guy in a dream that I could eat it? I love bacon!"

"I love bacon too, as long as it isn't loosey goosey. Enough about pork. You're making me hungry. Back to the angels. In Luke 1, the angel Gabriel told this wrinkly old man that he and his equally old wife were going to have a baby. The angel even told him to name the baby John. This baby grew up to be none other than . . . drum roll please . . . John the Baptist."

"But Dad, I've never heard God's real-life voice. Is it possible to actually hear Him?"

"Sure it is. The Bible tells about many people hearing God. Or in Saul's case, he heard Jesus speak even though Jesus wasn't actually there. You see, Saul was against Jesus and the disciples; he was trying to kill them. Well, as Saul was travelling with some men, Jesus appeared to him and spoke. He heard Jesus and all of his men heard Jesus, too. Then Saul went blind." Lily's dad covered his eyes. "That sure would get your attention." Acts 9

"If Jesus talked to me and then I couldn't see, I would listen too."

"Well, Saul got better a few days later, after the Lord spoke to another man named Ananias and told him to go find Saul. God practically gave Ananias the street address where Saul was staying." Acts 9

Lily giggled. "I know an even better lesson about hearing God."

"What's that?"

"The one when God spoke through a donkey. We learned it in Sunday school." Lily sat all the way up in bed. "A donkey was carrying this guy who was going to curse Moses and his friends. The donkey saw an angel with a sword standing in his way, so the donkey stopped. The rider slapped the donkey and made him go forward again. This happened two more times. On the third time, the donkey started speaking like a person and asked the man why he was beating him. The owner knew this was a message from God and instead of cursing Moses, he retold God's promises to those people."

"Yes, that's right. Balaam was his name and he was an evil man bribed to curse the Israelites. But after the run-in with the donkey, he gave prophecies of God's blessings to His chosen people." Numbers 22:21-Numbers 24:25

"Dad, I wish Bingo could speak and tell me what's right."

"Sweetie, it may not be that obvious and sometimes you may have to get into a quiet place to hear God. Elijah wanted to hear God, but there was a lot of noise and craziness around him. He had to go to a quiet place to hear Him. In fact, Elijah went to a cave. 1 Kings 19:11-13 Do you remember going into Ruby Falls cave last summer? Do you remember how dark and silent it was?"

Lily nodded. "I liked it down there. It felt comfy, like a cool hug."

"Well Elijah heard the soft voice of God in a cave. Sometimes we have so much noise going on around us, like the TV and the car radio playing. And if those things aren't distracting us, we have songs playing in our head. Like the ones I hear you singing while you brush your teeth. Sometimes we need to turn off the radio in the car . . . and the one in our head. When things are quiet, we can talk to and listen to God."

"What about those CDs we get from church? Should we turn those off too? Isn't it good to listen to the pastor's words?"

"Lilyana, you're right. Listening to Godly people is good. God speaks through others. In fact, you're more likely to hear God's voice through people than any other way. God has people help Him . . . and each other . . . that way. In fact, Jeremiah had God's words placed in his mouth." Jeremiah 1:9

"But Dad, how will I know if it's really God speaking through someone? What if they're lying, so people will listen to stuff that isn't true?"

"Good question. There are a few ways to tell the message is from God."

"Like what?"

"For one thing, the message will be timed perfectly. The person's message might answer questions you've been asking yourself and God. God's timing is always perfect. Let me think of an example . . . Well, in Acts 8, there was a guy from Ethiopia who was in charge of his queen's treasure. He was sitting in a chariot, reading a scripture. Philip happened to overhear the man reading and God told him to go speak to him. Imagine being sent by God to sit down next to someone really important at the mall food court."

Lily said, "Overheard him reading? I can read in my head and I'm just a kid."

"This guy was reading out loud because the words were in a different language and hard for him to understand. Philip asked if he understood the words. The man answered no, so Philip helped him understand the scripture. This opened the door for Philip to talk about Jesus. They started to travel together. Before they went their separate ways, Philip baptized him. The other man returned to his home in Ethiopia and spread God's word. This was God working. By telling this one super important guy, God was spreading the message about Jesus into Africa."

Lily asked, "Do you think God uses Pastor Tony to talk with us?"

"God definitely uses our pastor to talk to us. And sometimes I hear lyrics in a Christian song that seem to answer my prayers. You might get advice from friends, books, a teacher, or even a television show that is perfectly timed and fits exactly what you've been thinking about."

"But how will I know the message is really from God, besides the time? What if the people speaking are just lucky liars?"

"God's message will never go against the Bible or God's teachings. In the Bible, God tells us not to steal. If someone told you the right thing to do was to steal, the message wouldn't be from God."

"Okay, that makes sense." Lily scratched her ear. "What else?"

"God's message through others will always bring glory to God. It may come as a warning, a truth about our lives, or a blessing. But no matter what, when you hear the words, you'll know they're from God."

"I want God to warn me before bad things happen. What's that like?"

"Well, do you remember Joseph from the Bible?"

"Are we talkin' about Jesus' Dad or the guy with the colorful coat?"

"The one with the coat. Joseph was really good at interpreting dreams. He could figure out God's message from his own dreams and even understand other people's dreams. God gave him that gift. Through Joseph's dreams, God warned His people about the future. Joseph's gift for interpreting dreams even saved people from starving." Genesis 41

"That would be a cool gift."

"It is. Another guy named Daniel also had this gift from God. Daniel saved lives by interpreting a dream for King Nebuchadnezzar." Daniel 2:19

Lily squished her pillow. "So, God can talk to people by giving them a dream."

"Sure he can. In the book of Genesis, God gave King Abimelech a dream telling him to break up with the most beautiful woman because she was already married." Genesis 20:3

"Right Dad! God is giving dating advice now?"

"Sure He is. He talks with people all the time about how they should live their lives. Like when Jesus was at court for what they called crimes. Pilate was the Governor who had to decide if Jesus was guilty. The night before Jesus was put on the cross, Pilate's wife had a dream that Jesus was innocent. His wife even sent a message to her husband to try to save Jesus' life." Matthew 27:19

Lily asked, "Would the note from that guy's wife be a sign from God?"

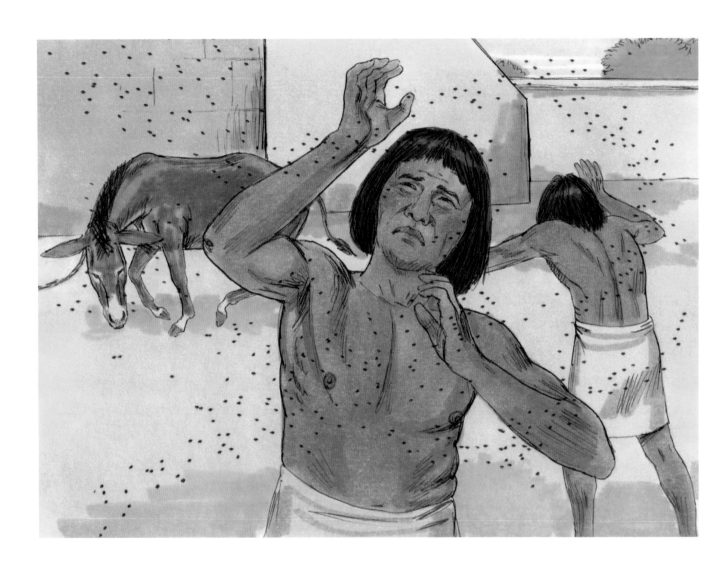

Lily's dad had to think for a minute. "No, not exactly. A sign from God might be something that gets your attention, but it will be followed up by some action. Like Moses and the Pharaoh. God sent signs like frogs, locusts, and bugs. But after those signs, God also sent Moses to tell Pharaoh he must free the Jews." Exodus 8 and 10

Lily said, "That's like the burning bush. The bush was just a sign to get Moses' attention, but God's words came after that." Exodus 3

"You're a smart girl!" Her dad smiled and rubbed her head. "You can find more of God's real messages in the Bible. This is why it's important to read the Bible."

"I tried to read your big Bible, but I didn't get it. If God was trying to speak to me, I didn't understand."

"Tomorrow, I'll buy you the <u>Easy To Read Bible</u>. You'll be able to understand it. As you choose what to read, don't just open the Bible and see what's there. First, think about God and imagine him moving your hand to find the parts He wants you to read. He can guide you to the things you're thinking about. God can help you hear His word about what's going on in your life, what's on your mind, what's bothering you."

"Dad, I can read the Bible all day long, but how will I know if God is talking to me?"

"If you pray about your problems, as you read, you may see that He is answering you through the words in the Bible. Once you've made a hard decision, a feeling of peace might rush over you. That's God's peace coming to you."

Lily's face lit up. "I've felt that before! Sometimes I just get a feeling that I should or should not do some things. Like when I forgave that bully. I was just lying in bed. My knee burned where it got scraped up. I prayed for my family and friends, like I usually do, and then I told God that I forgave that boy. Right then, I felt peaceful, like I was getting a hug." Lily's cheeks turned a little red. "That means God has been listening and I didn't even know it."

"Lily, that's God speaking. He can speak pretty loudly, even without words. God gives us all a sense of right and wrong. It is the Holy Spirit helping us to do the right thing, the Godly thing. The Bible refers to this as God's spirit living within us." 1 Corinthians 3:16

Lily sighed. "But I want to know He's really talking to me."

"Ask him to give you that gift. He promises it in the Bible. Joel 2:28 So ask Him to help you realize when He's talking to you. Daniel wrote down his dreams. You could do that, too." Daniel 7:1

"Maybe I could do that in my diary."

"Alright sweetie, it's night-night time. Let's say the Lord's Prayer. Matthew 6:9-13 You say a line and I'll translate what each line means."

"Okay, Dad." Lily folded her hands. "Our Father which art in heaven."

"I'm calling God here!"

"Hallowed be thy name."

"Your name will be holy to us."

"Thy kingdom come."

"Soon, heaven will be prepared for us."

"Thy will be done in earth."

"We pray that everything you want to happen on earth will happen."

"As it is in heaven."

"We also pray that everything you're preparing in heaven will also come true."

"Give us this day our daily bread."

"Please feed us. Feed our spirits and also fill our bellies, so we aren't starving."

"And forgive us our debts."

"Forgive me for the bad things I've done."

"As we forgive our debtors."

"God, forgive those people who have done bad things to us and made us feel bad, like that bully."

"And lead us not into temptation."

"There are bad choices all around us, pulling us away from You. Don't let me go down any bad paths."

"But deliver us from evil."

"Don't let the devil get me. Keep me safe."

"For thine is the kingdom, and the power, and the glory, forever."

"You control the kingdom. You have all the power. You deserve all the glory. God, you will have these things forever."

"Amen."

"You may be seated!"

"No Dad, that's not what Amen means!"

"Lily, that's what Pastor Tony says when he wants us to sit down."

"No, Amen means 'everything I prayed will happen.'"

"Lily, you are one of God's perfect children. You were born for a specific Godly purpose. God loves you."

As her father was walking out the door, Lily called out, "Dad, God loves you, too."

Made in the USA
San Bernardino, CA
29 September 2014